Original title:
The Foliage Festival

Copyright © 2025 Creative Arts Management OÜ
All rights reserved.

Author: Rafael Sterling
ISBN HARDBACK: 978-1-80567-018-6
ISBN PAPERBACK: 978-1-80567-098-8

Treading on a Golden Carpet

Golden leaves beneath my feet,
They whisper secrets, oh so sweet.
Squirrels snicker from the trees,
As I trip on roots with ease.

Pumpkins grinning, quite a sight,
Mischief lurking, day and night.
I'm a dancer on this ground,
While giggles echo all around.

Adventure in the Dappled Shadows

Dappled light through branches peek,
I chase a shadow, oh so sleek.
A chipmunk chuckles at my plight,
As I fumble in this light.

Leaves above like confetti fall,
I trip and stumble, feel so small.
Yet each tumble brings a cheer,
As nature's humor draws me near.

Rustling Revelations

Rustling leaves a chatter loud,
It feels like I'm in a playful crowd.
A breeze brings laughter, quick and bright,
As branches tickle, what a sight!

Nature's jesters tease and play,
With leafy pranks throughout the day.
My sneakers squeak, a funny sound,
In this vibrant playground found.

Petals Beneath the Maple

Petals drift from maple trees,
Like confetti dancing in the breeze.
I try to catch one, oh, so bold,
But every reach just leaves me cold.

Underneath a bright blue sky,
With laughter ringing, time flies by.
Each twist and turn, a surprise,
As petals fall and giggles rise.

Shadows of Orange and Brown

Leaves are falling, one by one,
Squirrels thinking, what a fun!
Grab a blanket, sip some tea,
Nature's show, oh look at me!

Pumpkins dancing on the ground,
Laughter echoes all around.
Children leap and twirl in glee,
Caught mid-jump in autumn spree.

Sweaters dragging, colors bright,
Hats that make you look a fright.
With each breeze, a silly chase,
Leaves like confetti, oh what grace!

On the ground, a leafy snack,
Crunching sounds, a pleasing crack.
Who needs corn when leaves abound?
Let's have fun on this leaf mound!

Reflections on Shimmering Waters

Ripples giggle, frogs take flight,
Jumping high, oh what a sight!
The geese are strutting, own the shore,
Splashing water, wanting more!

Bubbles rise like tiny dreams,
Fish play tag in secret streams.
Reflections dance on liquid glass,
We all wonder who will pass.

Colored leaves float, oh so bold,
A duck's new hat, bright orange gold.
Photos taken, smiles galore,
Splashing fun, let's ask for more!

The sunset's blush, a funny show,
Makes the water gleam and glow.
Who knew autumn had such flair?
Join the fun, a splash of air!

The Dance of Leafy Whispers

Leaves are prancing, don't be shy,
Look they twirl; oh my, oh my!
Branches sway, a leafy song,
Join their rhythm, you can't go wrong.

Mice in capes, having a ball,
Raccoons waltzing, who can call?
Here comes a breeze, it twirls and spins,
Nature's party, let's all join in!

Gusts of laughter, who will win?
Squirrels giggle, dive right in!
Dance with shadows, leap with flair,
Rustling secrets fill the air.

Twisting leaves, choreographed art,
Every flop, a work of heart.
So grab a partner, take a chance,
In this autumn leaf romance!

In Celebration of the Colorful Gifts

Nature's palette, bold and bright,
Brushes of gold in morning light.
Laughter bursts from every scene,
Who knew the woods could be so keen?

The acorns giggle, rolling free,
Hiding spot, oh can you see?
Mother Nature's silly stash,
Color and fun, a brisk little dash.

Gather 'round, the harvest calls,
with silly games in leafy halls.
The squirrels shout, play tag and run,
In this realm, we all have fun!

So let's rejoice, laugh, and sing,
In this splash of color, joy we bring.
For autumn's gifts are more than they seem,
A joyful festival, live the dream!

Whispers of Autumn's Tapestry

The leaves whisper tales of their flight,
As squirrels don capes made of light.
Pumpkins roll by with a giggle,
While acorns decide just to wiggle.

The trees toss their colors in glee,
While squirrels debate what to wear for tea.
A haystack laughs, full of dusty cheer,
As the wind scolds the clouds, 'Get out of here!'

Leaves in a Dance of Gold

In the park, the leaves start to sway,
Doing the limbo, hip-hop, and ballet.
A breeze throws a party, quite unplanned,
With twirling dancers, none can withstand.

The pumpkin patches are busting with jokes,
While scarecrows pretend to be clumsy folks.
The sun winks down, it's a cheeky fellow,
Painting the world with a laugh and a bellow.

Nature's Colorful Canvas

Paintbrushes dip in crimson and gold,
As nature giggles, never too old.
Each tree dons a hat that's wonderfully bright,
While crickets tell tales that tickle the night.

The sun throws a splash on the fields below,
As bunnies hop in a colorful show.
With every tickle of a wandering breeze,
The world becomes filled with laughter and ease.

Symphony of the Changers

A symphony brews in the crisp autumn air,
With rustling leaves performing with flair.
The squirrels add tambourines to the mix,
As the winds blow a whistle, quick as a fix.

The trees high-five with each gust that comes,
While acorns roll around, making drums.
Juggling pumpkins join in the fun,
As nature laughs, 'Oh, aren't we the ones!'

Harvest Moon's Gentle Glow

In the garden, pumpkins grin,
Waving at the moon's chagrin.
Squirrels stockpile, hoarding nuts,
While raccoons dance in polka huts.

Jack-o'-lanterns flicker bright,
Casting shadows, giving fright.
Ghosts of veggies roam the night,
While the owls in robes take flight.

Serenade of the Swaying Branches

Leaves do the cha-cha on the breeze,
Acorns drop like clumsy keys.
Chirping crickets hold a show,
As branches sway to a silly flow.

Birds gossip in the morning light,
Birdseed party, what a sight!
Squirrels bicker, tails afluff,
Nature's soap opera, isn't life tough?

A Walk Through Brushstrokes of Autumn

Walking through an artist's scene,
Nature's colors, a playful green.
The maples blush, the oaks just laugh,
Chasing each other down the path.

Windswept leaves dance all around,
Whispering secrets with their sound.
A playful breeze tugs at my hat,
While I trip over a fat, silly cat.

Secrets of the Dappled Path

On the trail where shadows play,
Frogs wear crowns, hippos sway.
Mushrooms giggle, tickled by rain,
As earthworms wiggle, free from pain.

Sunbeams laugh through branches high,
Tickling hedgehogs passing by.
Every step's a quirky find,
In this circus for the mind.

Journeys Through Charmed Woods

In woods where squirrels wear hats,
A raccoon serenades with spats.
Leaves laugh as they twirl and dance,
Each step brings a leaf's new chance.

Bunnies bounce on pumpkin trails,
Telling tales of long-lost fails.
Mushrooms peek from underbrush,
While the snails start to giddily rush.

Trees gossip in rustling tones,
Whispers of mischief, jokes, and puns.
Acorns fall like little grenades,
As critters plan their playful raids.

Through branches swaying left and right,
A chipmunk channels pure delight.
The woods are a carnival spree,
Join the fun, wild and free!

A Festival of Changing Dreams

Under the canopy, dreams take flight,
Leaves in costumes, a hilarious sight.
With each flutter, a new joke shared,
Who knew that trees could be so daring?

Pumpkins giggle as they roll about,
Spilling seeds with a playful shout.
Squirrels strut in fancy dress,
Chasing acorns, a funny mess.

Clouds above make faces too,
Changing shapes, they join the crew.
Breezes whisper, tickle and tease,
Everything's silly, none are at ease.

In this wild, whimsical cheer,
Nature's laughter rings loud and clear.
So come, let your worries escape,
Join the merriment, reshape your fate!

Embracing Autumn's Haunting Beauty

As the trees shed their leafy crowns,
Crows in costumes parade through towns.
Ghostly apparitions with orange glow,
Dance in circles, putting on a show.

Pies on windowsills start to sing,
While mischievous raccoons try to fling,
Apple bobbing with pumpkins near,
Filling the air with joyous cheer.

A crisp wind carries laughter bright,
Turtlenecks and mittens, the style of night.
Chasing shadows that giggle and glide,
In this haunting, we can't help but bide.

Celebrate this lovely plight,
Where every corner brings pure delight.
Laughter lingers as leaves take flight,
Embrace the charm of autumn's height!

When Leaves Turn to Gold

In shades of red, the trees do blush,
Squirrels debate, "Is it time to rush?"
They gather nuts with playful grins,
While acorns drop like some grand sins.

The ground's a carpet, a crunchy thrill,
Every step's a crackle, a joyous spill.
Boots dance around in a swirling spree,
As nature laughs and jubilantly frees.

Embrace of the Changing Season

Pumpkins sit like hats on the ground,
The wind makes whispers, a playful sound.
A scarecrow yawns, it's seen too much,
Waving his arms like he's lost his touch.

Bees are buzzing, but they're just so tired,
Finding their rhythm, though slightly inspired.
Flowers bow low, then toss their heads,
"Is it winter soon?" they wonder in spreads.

Chronicles of the Leafy Realm

In the kingdom of trees, the leaves conspire,
Whispering secrets, they never tire.
"Autumn's here, let's paint the sky!"
They giggle and rustle, oh my, oh my!

A branch complained, "I'm feeling bare!"
While another shouted, "I don't care!"
With each little leaf taking flight in glee,
They swirl about like a fancy tea!

Harvesting the Colors of Change

Cider flows like rivers, sweet and bold,
Trees rustle their tales, ancient and old.
Mice dance under moonlight, quite absurd,
While pumpkins sing, oh how we've heard!

Caramel apples sit on a stand,
With toothy grins, they're in high demand.
Goblins and ghouls prepare for the night,
Celebrating the harvest, all in delight.

Threads of Amber and Crimson

Leaves dance down like giggling clowns,
In swirls and twirls, they wear bright gowns.
The trees, they chuckle, a leafy jest,
As squirrels prance in their fluffy vest.

Pumpkins grinning with toothy smiles,
Join in the fun, they stretch for miles.
The wind plays tag, it tugs at our hats,
While acorns roll, like chubby little cats.

Portraits in Shifting Hues

Canvas of colors, splashed so bright,
Nature's palette bursts into light.
Critters pose for an artful glance,
As branches sway in a silly dance.

A robin's laugh, a chipmunk's cheer,
Echoes of joy, all around here.
The world wears orange, gold, and green,
With every step, a new scene is seen.

Enchanted Grove Celebration

In a grove where giggles echo wide,
Mushrooms wear hats, a fungal pride.
The owls wink with knowing eyes,
As fairy lights twinkle like fireflies.

Tiny creatures with tiny feet,
Have a dance-off that's quite a treat.
With bits of acorn and maple syrup,
Even the trees sway with a hip-hop hiccup.

The Laughter of Rustling Leaves

Leaves whisper secrets in the breeze,
Tickling the branches, swaying with ease.
A leaf falls here, a leaf falls there,
Each plop a punchline, we stop and stare.

With laughter blooming in crisp, cool air,
A playful spirit, everywhere.
Chasing shadows, we run and leap,
In this leafy realm, joy runs deep.

Rustling Reveries of Fall

Leaves tumble down like a clumsy dance,
Squirrels steal acorns, pondering their chance.
The wind whispers secrets, a leafy parade,
While pumpkins watch over, their orange charade.

Children in sweaters, too big for their frame,
Chase after wishes, not caring for fame.
The crunching of leaves is a symphonic cheer,
As laughter rings out, autumn's song crystal clear.

The Painted Pathway of Seasons

Trees wear colors, a dazzling spree,
Maple and oak in bright jubilee.
The pathways are carpeted, nature's delight,
With hues of joy, each step feels just right.

Young critters gather, sharing their snacks,
Racing through leaves, no time for a pact.
They tumble and roll, in a whirlwind of fun,
Their foliage playground, a race to be done.

Harvesting Hues in Harmony

Oranges, reds, and yellows collide,
Fruitful adventures where chuckles reside.
Baking apple pies that smell so divine,
While the pumpkin gets carved with a goofy design.

The scarecrow giggles, his shirt full of holes,
As cornstalks sway gently, they playfully stroll.
Nature's big canvas, a bright merry scene,
Harvesting hues, a feast fit for queens!

The Woven Blanket of Time

Threads of gold and amber weave through the air,
Time's cozy quilt, made with glee and care.
Each stitch a chuckle, each patch a jest,
As the world dons layers, nature's fest.

Couples with cider, sharing sweet sips,
Wrapped in the laughter, their joy takes trips.
Underneath branches that stretch and sway,
Life's funny moments gather and play.

Golden Confetti from the Sky

Leaves dance down like giggling sprites,
Spinning in air, oh what great sights!
Squirrels in hats throw tiny snacks,
While birds wear shades and plot their tracks.

Sunshine winks through branches wide,
Bouncing off puddles, oh what a ride!
A gusty breeze sends hats a-twirling,
As laughter echoes, the joy is unfurling.

Secrets of the Whispering Branches

Branches gossip with rustling tones,
Sharing tales of acorns and stones.
Chattering leaves reveal their tricks,
As bushes giggle with little flicks.

A raccoon wearing a tiny bow,
Plans mischief with a cheeky glow.
In this woodland, secrets not few,
Every nook is alive, brimming anew.

Pumpkin Spice and Maple Kisses

Brewed aromas drift through the air,
Pumpkin spice lattes without a care.
Maples do wink with their syrupy smiles,
As critters appear wearing autumnal styles.

A dancing fox in a scarf so bright,
Pirouettes past owls with wisdom and sight.
Every sip tastes of golden delight,
While squirrels toast under twinkling light.

Echoes of the Enchanted Grove

Echoes bounce from tree to tree,
As nature giggles, oh so free.
A bear breaks out in a silly dance,
While butterflies join in a swirling prance.

Glowworms sing with voices sweet,
Twirling mid-air on tiny feet.
In this grove where wonders thrive,
Every laugh feels so alive!

A Serenade Underneath Scarlet Canopies

Beneath the trees, we dance and prance,
With leaves like confetti, it's quite a chance.
Squirrels stare, judging our moves,
While we shake our limbs to the music grooves.

A bird drops a twig, it lands on my head,
Laughter erupts as we feel misled.
'Free decor!' we cheer, adjusting our flair,
Who knew nature had a delightful affair?

Umbrellas of Orange and Brown

As we stroll through this crunchy land,
Each step's a crackle, oh, isn't it grand?
With leaves overhead like a patchwork quilt,
We dodge raindrops of brown, our skills are built.

A rogue gust flies, whoosh goes my hat,
It spins like a frisbee, imagine that!
We chase it down like it's a game,
While nearby trees chuckle, feeling no shame.

Twilight Tales of Leafy Whispers

As twilight falls, the shadows tease,
Leaves whisper secrets in the chilly breeze.
Crickets chirp, telling jokes from the ground,
While owls roll their eyes, not a sound around.

A raccoon plays tag, stealing our snacks,
While we fumble and trip, avoiding attacks.
We laugh and we squeal, stuck in a twig,
Inventing wild antics, like we're all big.

Chasing Shadows Through the Canopy

Through layers of leaves, we leap and bound,
Each shadow a friend, so clever and round.
We seek out the mist, and play hide-and-seek,
While the moon rolls its eyes, trying not to peek.

A dance-off breaks out, with twirls and spins,
Until I trip over roots – where's my wins?
My friends laugh and tumble, in joyful dismay,
Amongst the cool shadows, we savor the play.

Leaves of Reflection

In the park, the leaves dance,
Falling down in a curious trance.
Squirrels chime with all their might,
Chasing shadows, what a sight!

Golden hues, a true delight,
Piling up, they reach great height.
In a pile, I take a leap,
Dodging mud, it's fun to sweep!

Each leaf whispers a cheeky joke,
Twirling down like a silly folk.
Nature laughs, it plays along,
A rustling chorus, a joyful song.

With every gust, the giggles rise,
Nature's jest amidst the skies.
So grab a leaf, let's all collide,
In this madness, we'll take pride!

Gathering in Leaves' Warm Embrace

Gather round the leafy mound,
With laughter echoing all around.
Children scoff, a giddy spree,
As leaves swirl like it's jubilee!

A great big mess, chaos reigns,
Fluffy hats and muddy stains.
In each pile, a treasure lies,
A hidden gem beneath the skies.

We stomp and jump, a playful race,
Foliage fluffs in our embrace.
Who knew grass could tickle feet,
While chatting like it's such a treat?

Silly hats and bright attire,
These golden crowns we all desire.
In nature's chat, we share a grin,
For in this fun, we all win!

The Essence of Earthly Beauty

Oh! The hues of orange and red,
They tease the eyes, a feast ahead.
With each flutter, a chuckle grows,
As autumn winds play with our nose!

A leaf fell, oh, what a dive!
Splat! The laughter comes alive.
Grass stains on my favorite jeans,
A reminder of these autumn scenes.

Spinning round in joyful bliss,
Catching leaves, oh, what a miss!
Nature's marbles, bright and sound,
In this madness, joy is found.

We'll sip hot cider, cozy, warm,
While leaves above perform their charm.
A playful dance, a leaf parade,
In every twirl, a vibrant trade!

A Tapestry of Twisting Vines

In the thicket, vines entwine,
Twisting tales both bold and fine.
Chasing critters, they play tag,
While hanging low, they start to brag!

Leaves invite the ants to crawl,
As they build little leaf-filled halls.
A twisting maze, a leafy quest,
In viney wraps, we're truly blessed.

Juggling fruits that drop with flair,
Oops, I've sneezed – a fruit affair!
With each bounce, a giggle spreads,
As berries tumble on our heads.

In this green maze, we prance about,
Laughing loud, there's little doubt.
A tapestry, we weave with glee,
This playful nature, wild and free!

Dancers Beneath Rustling Boughs

Leaves sway like they know the dance,
Roots tapping with a silly prance.
Squirrels giggle as they leap,
Nature's party, no time for sleep.

Branches shimmy in the breeze,
Acorns tumble down like peas.
Bugs wearing hats dance in a line,
Spinning around like they're sipping wine.

Grasshoppers join with flashy moves,
Each hop a cheer that surely soothes.
Even the sun peeks through the leaves,
Chuckling softly, as the world believes.

Frogs croak jokes from mossy logs,
While clever owls act like snogs.
With every rustle, laughter grows,
In this giggle-fest the whole world knows.

Symphony of Colors Unleashed

Crimson leaves laugh, waving bright,
Yellows twirl, what a sight!
Greens wear shades of mischief, too,
Nature's palette, a giddy crew.

Orange leaves wiggle, making sound,
As purple ones bounce from ground.
A burst of hues, a vibrant yelp,
It's a clownish scheme, oh what a help!

Butterflies wear their fanciest threads,
As insects drop by, spinning heads.
With each flutter, a chorus sings,
A whimsical tune, oh how it clings.

Raccoons tiptoe, taking a peek,
Caught in colors, not a word to speak.
A riot of shades prances about,
In this carnival, there's no doubt.

Nature's Tapestry Unfurled

Woven threads of green and gold,
Tales of laughter, brightly told.
Birds perform a silly play,
Wings flapping in a jazzy way.

Stitching paths of crunching leaves,
A tapestry that just believes.
Squirrels weaving in and out,
Playing tag, there's never doubt!

In the fabric, sunlight gleams,
A quilt of joy, woven dreams.
Each colour hides a funny tale,
Spirited whispers on the gale.

Pine cones dance, rolling with glee,
While shadows chuckle, can you see?
In this forest's vibrant arc,
Life's a lark, and laughter's the spark.

Kaleidoscope of Nature's Bounty

Step right up, the show begins,
Pine needles giggle, laughter spins.
Nutty acorns roll and tumble,
Nature's circus, never humble.

Berries burst in vibrant hues,
Like candy for the forest muse.
With every fruit, a joke unfolds,
A chuckle shared, a story told.

Check those mushrooms, wiggly and round,
Mimicking grins from the damp ground.
While breezes whisper cheeky rhymes,
Nature's jesters, on borrowed times.

Leaves perform their cheeky waltz,
As nature sometimes takes the faults.
In this patch of mischief-free,
Laughter blooms—come party with me!

Mosaics in the Woodland Light

Colors splashed on branches wide,
Squirrels chuckling, trying to hide,
Leaves gossip like old friends so dear,
Nature's jokes ring loud and clear.

A beetle waltzes on a twig,
Sipping dew like it's a wig,
Mushrooms pose in silly hats,
As crickets sing their witty chats.

A chipmunk struts with acorn pride,
Winking at the world outside,
Underneath the trees so bright,
A playful dance, what a sight!

Whispers of the forest tease,
Every rustle, steeped in ease,
Together laugh, the fauna cheer,
In this light, fun is always near.

A Canopy of Stories

In the branches, tales unfold,
Birds narrate of treasures bold,
A raccoon with a penchant fine,
Steals the show, he's simply divine.

Once a squirrel missed his flight,
Landed in a pumpkin bright,
There he rolled, a sight so grand,
As laughter spread across the land.

A fox rehearses lines robust,
In the spotlight, he can trust,
With every rustle, whispers swell,
The trees hold secrets they won't tell.

As sunbeams shine on leaf and bark,
Nature's stage is set for a spark,
And every critter plays their part,
In the woods, it's a work of art.

Golden Hour Among the Trees

Golden rays paint trunks with glee,
Bugs embroiled in a math spree,
Counting leaves as they're swirled down,
A whimsical quest in the town.

The shadows stretch like a cat's yawn,
While critters are planning their dawn,
A deer stumbles, knocks over glades,
As laughter echoes, the sunlight fades.

Beneath the glow, a turtle grins,
Wearing moss like it's silk, wins,
A rabbit relies on silly rhymes,
To break through the autumn climes.

Every rustle, a clue to find,
Moments shared with joys intertwined,
As evening falls, their giggles rise,
Underneath the painted skies.

The Dance of Falling Leaves

Leaves are twirling, spinning round,
Each one falls with a gentle sound,
Raccoons huddle in their festoon,
Underneath the chortling moon.

A leaf slips, does a silly roll,
While a gull opens its big old hole,
Mimicking the way they drift and dive,
Every slip gives giggles alive.

Chirping crickets hum along,
As twigs get down, they join the song,
Even clumps of grass decide it's time,
To bop along, oh so sublime!

With every breeze, a whimsy tease,
Painting laughter through the trees,
Autumn's stage, a lively scene,
Where nature reigns and giggles glean.

Twilight in the Woodland Whirl

In tights of brown and gold, they dance,
   Little squirrels in a leafy trance.
They tumble down with sprightly cheer,
   As acorns roll, they shed a tear.

With twigs like wands, they wave their paws,
   An audience of owls with silent jaws.
The moon peeks in with a wry grin,
   As shenanigans rumble from within.

Beneath the crickle-crackle scene,
   A berry pie is sight unseen.
A raccoon sneaks, with mischief rife,
   Swiping snacks for woodland life.

As twilight falls, the shadows play,
   Nature's jesters come out to sway.
They giggle and hoot, in jest they dwell,
   In this funny world, all is well.

Counting the Shades of Autumn

There's red, there's gold, then comes the brown,
Colors that whirl, and tumble down.
A pile of leaves just caught my eye,
Who knew they loved to frolic and fly?

Each shade a character, quite a sight,
With flaming orange, they start a fight.
The yellows giggle, the browns they jest,
Under a tree, it's an autumn fest.

They gather around for a leaf parade,
With twirling stems, quite a charade.
The crunch underfoot, a route so grand,
With every step, they take a stand.

So here's to hues, all jolly and bright,
Counting the shades in the dusky light.
With quips and jibes, they paint the ground,
In laughter and color, joy is found.

Leafy Lullabies in the Breeze

Hush now, the leaves begin to hum,
In rusty whispers, they strum and strum.
Twirling in circles, what a sight,
A leafy choir taking flight.

With every gust, they sway and glide,
Chasing the wind in a joyful ride.
They tickle the branches, dance on the ground,
In this frolicsome symphony, joy is found.

A squirrel hops by with its acorn stash,
Testing if the winds are feeling brash.
Then off it scurries, in leaps and bounds,
Amidst the laughter of nature's sounds.

So listen close to their leafy song,
In the bustling shade where the critters belong.
From twig to twig, the giggles tease,
In this woodland lull, life's a breeze.

Beneath the Flourish of Canopies

Under the leaves where the shadows play,
Lies a gopher with not much to say.
He grumbles and grunts with a cheeky grin,
Claiming his turf while the leaf piles spin.

A group of ants march in a line,
With crumbs on their backs, they're feeling fine.
They stumble and tumble, drop a crumb,
"Back to the queen, come on, don't be glum!"

Up in the branches, the crows conspire,
Flinging gossip like a feathered choir.
"Did you see that jump? That was a sight!"
"Bet you can't top me, come on, take flight!"

So gather round, in this giggling glade,
Where nature's critters have all made trade.
Under the bright and rustling trees,
Life's little jokes float like a breeze.

Whispers of the Honeyed Breeze

Leaves giggle as they fall,
Tickling the noses of us all.
Squirrels dance in their acorn hats,
Chasing shadows and silly chats.

Pumpkin spice in the air sings,
Even the trees are trying new things.
A raccoon with a mask takes a bow,
What a sight! We all laugh out loud.

Crisp apples roll on the ground,
While chirpy birds make a ruckus around.
The breeze brings whispers, sweet and light,
As neighbors feign fright at a leaf's flight.

In this carnival of gold and brown,
You'll find laughter all over town.
With nature as the party's host,
We toast to the joy we love most!

Gathering Beneath Autumn's Gaze

Under the trees, we gather and cheer,
With pumpkins and laughter, there's nothing to fear.
Jumping in leaves, a crunchy delight,
Our giggles echo from morning 'til night.

A scarecrow grins, doing the twist,
His dance moves leave no room for a miss.
Who knew that corn could be so clever?
This fun in the fields? It should last forever!

Hot cider flows like a river of cheer,
But watch your step—those apples are near!
Oh, look! A raccoon with a gourd in his paws,
Such antics and joy deserve loud applause!

Gathering folks from far and wide,
Autumn has invited us all for a ride.
With smiles so big, and hearts open wide,
In this merry moment, we take great pride.

Scenic Fête of the Changing Leaves

In a magical land where the color's a blast,
We twirl and we spin, oh, the fun and the fast!
Leaves like confetti float down to the ground,
While laughter and joy are the best of the sound.

A fox wearing socks and his hat far too low,
Trips over branches, puts on quite a show.
Pumpkin parades march down the street,
Each float a dance that none can beat!

Bobbing bobbing on inflatable gourds,
Chasing squirrels as they gather their hoards.
The crows hold a meeting, debating a plan,
While we munch on popcorn, a festival clan.

Giggles and whispers, the air full of dreams,
As children play tag near the bubbling streams.
With no room for frowns in this colorful maze,
We'll all remember these golden days!

Heartbeats of a Forest Transformed

In a forest where giggles dart and weave,
Whispers of mischief in every leaf.
A bear in a tutu does pirouettes,
While all the pine trees place silly bets.

Fruits of the season, plump and round,
On fence posts, the cutest raccoons abound.
The owls hoot tunes, the squirrels provide beats,
As nature's party just cannot be beat!

Fog rolls in with a cloak of surprise,
Leaving us peeking with wide-open eyes.
Mushrooms in hats dance under the moon,
What a wild evening! We'll be here till noon.

The forest now pulses with rhythms of glee,
Each critter a dancer, a trickster, a spree.
As night falls, laughter rings through the trees,
In this transformed woodland, we find our ease.

Conversations Among the Canopy

The leaves all whisper, oh what a chat,
A squirrel interrupts, with a cheeky splat.
"Did you see the acorn?" one leaf did say,
"I think it was stolen, right from our sway!"

The branches are laughing, swaying in glee,
While a bird swoops low, saying, "Look at me!"
"You call that a dance? Such clumsy confetti!"
A twig adds, "Dear friend, your moves are quite petty!"

Dancing clouds peek in, they giggle and stare,
As the breezy winds tease and toss through the air.
"Oh, what joys we share, in this lofty retreat!"
Leaves wave their green arms, counting each heartbeat.

But wait! A raindrop, a sudden surprise!
The leaves all shout out, with wide-open eyes.
"Duck and cover! It's time to take flight!"
The canopy chuckles, aglow with delight!

Roots in a Canvas of Change

Down below, the roots weave tales untold,
A dandelion giggles, say, "Aren't we bold?"
"Shake off that dust, we're set to explore!"
Cries a root, as they stretch, seeking more!

With twirls of mud, they dance in the grime,
"Let's prank the flowers, we'll give them a rhyme!"
A daisy bemused exclaims, "Oh please, no!"
But the roots just laugh, "We won't take it slow!"

Suddenly a worm winks, says, "Join my parade!"
All roots are now laughing, their worries all fade.
"We're part of the canvas, each twist, curve, and bend,
Let's make sure our stories never will end!"

In this jolly dance, time starts to spin,
Each bump, each roughed edge, a story within.
With quirks and with giggles, they dig even deeper,
Roots in a canvas, becoming a keeper!

Nature's Festive Cloak

Wrapped in hues of red and bright sunny yellows,
Nature dons layers, nothing but fellows.
A pumpkin rolls by, with a grin on its face,
"Where's my invite? I want in on the race!"

The acorns all chuckle, with their caps held so high,
"Look at our outfits! We're ready to fly!"
One leaf takes a bow, shouting, "I'm quite grand!"
While a beetle proclaims, "I'm the star of the band!"

A chorus of crickets strikes up a loud tune,
The sun-warmed tomatoes join in with a swoon.
"Oh, bring on the fruits, let's toast with delight!"
With laughter and chatter, they party all night!

As daylight fades out, the moon starts to glow,
The festive cloak twirls, with a whimsical flow.
Under twinkling stars, they dance with pure glee,
Nature's grand evening, a wild jubilee!

Parading the Vibrant Palette

The colors take flight, a parade on the breeze,
"Hey, look at me! I'm the shade of fresh peas!"
An orange leaf shouts, "I'm bright and I'm bold!"
Green giggles back, "You look like old mold!"

They prance through the fields, a marvelous scene,
Purple gets dizzy, spinning pure green.
"Let's hide from the winds, let's sneak through the grass!"

They laugh at each other, while time seems to pass.

A jolly bouquet jumps, wears hats made of sass,
"Isn't this fun? Who can top our class?"
A butterfly drifts in, waving her wings,
"Come join my jubilee, oh, the joy that it brings!"

With each budding bloom, a new story is spun,
Colors collide, in this joyous fun run.
No frowns here, just smiles under sun's doting rays,
Parading the palette, in hilarious ways!

Flickers of Autumn Magic

Orange leaves in the air,
Dancing like they don't care.
Squirrels plotting a big heist,
Stealing acorns, oh so nice!

Frogs in hats croak with glee,
Sipping tea beneath a tree.
Pumpkins rolling down the street,
All of nature's kind of sweet!

Wind whispers jokes too bright,
Making trees sway left and right.
The harvest moon starts to tease,
Laughing at the swaying leaves.

Jackets come out, what a sight,
Hats funny, but just feels right.
Let's jump in piles, oh so high,
Chasing laughter till we cry!

Letters from the Leaf-Packed Earth

Leaves are scribbling their best notes,
Whispering secrets like old boats.
Brown ones tell tales of the past,
Green ones, stories that fly fast.

Nutty gossip in the air,
Rabbits chase, without a care.
Mushrooms giggle in a line,
While hedgehogs sip on dandelion wine.

Children laugh and dance around,
As swirling colors hit the ground.
Nature's mailman brings us cheer,
With every leaf that wanders near.

Who knew trees could joke like this?
With every rustle, laughter's bliss.
Each brown letter, a comic feat,
In this postal of autumn treat!

The Time of Giving Thanks

Gravy boats that gleam and glow,
Wish they could dance and put on a show.
Turkey struts with a feathered grin,
Saying, 'I hope I won't end up in a pin!'

The table's set with a funny flair,
Grandma winks with her silly hair.
Cousins giggle, share their tales,
About the kids who swiped the bales.

Pumpkin pie stacked way too high,
Everyone wants to give it a try.
'Who ate the last piece?' we all pout,
But laughter's the feast we can't live without!

Thankfulness spilled like the wine,
As we toast with a smile so fine.
Meals may end, but love will stay,
In this funny, festive display!

Cider, Sunlight, and Shimmering Leaves

Cider bubbling, a warm embrace,
Sunshine dances with playful grace.
Leaves twirl down, a colorful spree,
As if the trees are laughing with glee.

Bubbling like a cheerful brook,
Every sip holds a secret book.
Cinnamon sticks in a joyful stir,
Awakening joy that won't deter.

Jumping in piles, all in a rush,
Raking leaves turns into a crush.
Every child with a gleeful cheer,
Brings echoes of joy that all can hear.

As sunset paints the sky in gold,
Nature's stories are warmly told.
With cider in hand, let's dance and sway,
In the shimmer of leaves, we laugh and play!

Mosaics of Melancholy and Joy

Leaves tumble down with a playful flair,
Crunching beneath shoes, oh what a scare!
Colors collide in a feathery sweep,
Why does the squirrel seem lost in his leap?

Pumpkin spice lattes, a sip just for fun,
When did a latte become such a pun?
Sweaters emerge like a warm bear's hug,
But guess who forgot to check for the snug?

The scarecrow's a model with clothes in a twist,
Dancing in fields, he's the autumnist!
Chatting with crows, what do they say?
Gathering gossip about harvest day.

And when twilight giggles, the shadows align,
Hit the dance floor, it's grape juice and wine!
The crunch of the leaves, a whimsical tune,
As we twirl beneath the mischievous moon.

The Gentle Fall of Nature's Tears

Raindrops giggle as they tap on the ground,
Whispering secrets, an echoing sound.
The trees hold umbrellas, making a stand,
While the worms are all glittering, gleefully bland.

Little puddles form tiny new lakes,
And ducks throw a party while the sun wakes.
In coats too big, we splash with a cheer,
Carefree, we laugh, embracing the smear.

Socks get drenched, but who cares anyway?
The fun in the rain is just child's play.
A soggy old dog offers hugs from his fur,
While raindrops dance, like they think we're a blur.

And just like that, the clouds drift away,
Sunlight appears, brightening the gray.
With a wink and a shout, oh look at those fruits!
The silliness blooms in nature's cute boots.

Harvest Moon and Sapphire Skies

Beneath a round moon that's wearing a grin,
The pumpkins are plotting, let the fun begin!
Scarecrows are laughing, they're having a ball,
While unsuspecting rabbits take heed of their call.

Cider is bubbling in jugs on the floor,
With a sprinkle of laughter, it's never a bore.
The pies start to wink, as spices all blend,
Let's dig in, my friends, hold on to your trend!

Sapphire skies twinkle, a backdrop so fine,
Fireflies gossip what stars might align.
We dance with the moonbeams, our shadows do sway,
In this harvest of humor, we're never cliché.

And twilight arrives with a playful reminder,
That each autumn night gets just a little kinder.
Nature invites us to revel and roam,
In laughter and joy, let us call this our home.

A Dance with the Twilight Breezes

The breezes come swirling, a cheeky ballet,
Tickling the leaves in a feathery play.
Whirling around, they can't keep their place,
And I join their waltz, with pure goofy grace.

The sunset's a canvas of orange and pink,
With coy little clouds that begin to wink.
Just like a party with snacks on the side,
Each gust brings a giggle we cannot abide.

Chasing our shadows, we leap and we bound,
While whispers of twilight sweep softly around.
What's that in the distance? A ruckus, a cheer!
Oh, let's join the fun as the night draws near!

And as laughter mingles with stars up above,
Let's cherish this moment, this tangy sweet love.
Holding on to joy as the moon starts to rise,
In the dance of the breezes, we find our surprise.

The Art of Letting Go

Trees wear jackets, bright and bold,
Dancing leaves, a sight to behold.
With every gust, they swirl and prance,
It's nature's very own silly dance.

Squirrels are prepping for their grand feast,
While the birds complain, to say the least.
A leaf slips down, a graceful dive,
Laughing at the ground, saying, "I thrive!"

The ground's a carpet, a crunchy sound,
Where nature's laughter can truly be found.
Embrace the dirt, don't fight the fall,
Letting go is a trick, after all!

So twirl with the leaves, embrace the jest,
In this grand show, we're all just guests.
So join the fun, don't be a slowpoke,
Fall with splendor, and share a good joke.

Glimpse of Golden Horizons

A rustling whisper from the tree's peak,
Gold and red, it's a colorful streak.
Birds bicker over the best view,
Who knew horizons could dazzle so true?

Jumping through leaves like a playful sprite,
Chasing shadows in the glorious light.
Someone trips, and laughter fills the air,
Oops, let's hope no one spots that flair!

Maple syrup dreams on a sticky day,
Pancakes dropping, oh what a way!
Sipping cider, sipping cheer,
We'll toast to fall; the best time of year!

In golden hues, we dance and sing,
So much joy, just watching the bling.
Each glint a giggle, each hue a smile,
Join this adventure, let's stay a while!

Whispers of Autumn Leaves

Leaves chatter softly, secrets to weave,
Telling tales as they quit the eve.
A light breeze chuckles, a playful tease,
Dancing around like it's trying to please.

One leaf, it teases, slips on a vine,
"Catch me if you can" begins the design.
A swirl and a twirl, oh what a race,
As laughter erupts, it's quite the embrace!

Caterpillars gossip, plotting to fly,
While crickets chirp, "Oh me, oh my!"
The air is filled with a giggly delight,
As critters unite for this fleeting sight.

So let's whisper softly with every breeze,
Nature's funny side brings us to our knees.
Dive in the colors, let worries flee,
For autumn's a joke that sets us all free!

Celebration in Gilded Canopy

Under the canopy, the party is grand,
Leaves popping like confetti, all across the land.
A squirrel wears a hat, so dapper and bright,
Claiming the title of festive delight.

Rabbits are bouncing, shaking their tails,
Chasing the wind, leaving giggling trails.
Who knew such fun lurked in the trees?
A festival of laughter carried on the breeze!

Chipmunks are chefs with acorns to spare,
Cooking up mischief, sprinkles of flair.
Join the fun, sip some nectar divine,
Under this wonder, there's laughter and wine!

So here's to the canopy, lush and alive,
Where even the grumpy old owls will jive.
Let joy reign supreme, in this woodland spree,
Celebration abounding, come dance with me!

Ember Trails Through the Woods

In the woods, a squirrel took flight,
Chasing shadows in daylight.
He tripped on leaves, what a sight!
Even trees laughed with delight.

A raccoon in a top hat pranced,
As acorns rolled, he danced,
He bowed to owls, who glanced,
Nature's party, all entranced.

A fox with shades, quite absurd,
Said, "You never heard a bird?"
Each feather worn like a word,
In the absurdity, we stirred.

With every turn, surprises greet,
A field of mushrooms, quite the feat.
A fairy's hat, what a treat!
In these woods, we won't retreat.

A Tapestry of Crimson Dreams

Leaves tumble down, a jolly race,
A bear with a scarf, quite the face!
He rolled in reds, a messy place,
Wrapped in laughter, he found his space.

A crow in shades, so high and cool,
Cawed a tune, played the fool.
Swaying branches, nature's school,
Where every critter breaks the rule.

Pumpkins grinned from ear to ear,
Joined the fun, spread autumn cheer.
They said, "Come on, let's persevere!"
In this patch, there's nothing to fear.

With a zoom, a snail won the race,
A trophy made of spun pure lace.
All gathered round to give him grace,
In this wild, colorful space.

The Kaleidoscope of Nature's Breath

Under azure skies, leaves twirl and sway,
A chameleon wore a bright bouquet.
It danced and pranced, come what may,
In an ever-changing ballet.

In the thicket, a hedgehog spun,
With twigs and leaves, oh what fun!
It claimed, "Never can I run!"
Yet laughed as it basked in the sun.

Crickets chirped a silly tune,
As butterflies flirted with the moon.
"Watch us twirl!" they sang in June,
Nature's jesters, a colorful boon.

A fox painted red, with flair so bright,
Joined the fest under twinkling light.
In this party, all felt right,
In laughter's grip, we took flight.

In the Embrace of Decaying Beauty

In a garden of brown, a snail took a pause,
Admiring the charm of nature's flaws.
"It's merely decay!" said the hearty applause,
As crickets held court with their quirky laws.

The sunflowers bowed, a polka-dot crowd,
With petals that waved, drawing in a shroud.
Nearby, a frog croaked loud and proud,
Claiming the title of 'king' of the cloud.

A wise old tree told jokes of the past,
Said, "I've seen leaves both withered and vast."
With laughter erupting, the shadows were cast,
Every moment cherished, too good to last.

As laughter echoed, the world felt a shift,
Finding joy in decay, a natural gift.
In each rusty crinkle, our spirits would lift,
Embracing the season, time's funny drift.

Illuminated by Nature's Paintbrush

Leaves dance like confetti in the breeze,
Squirrels wear their acorn hats with ease.
Trees flaunt colors like a fashion show,
While owls gossip about the latest glow.

Pinecones roll like troops on parade,
Caterpillars dream of the plans they made.
Crickets throw parties with tunes so sweet,
And mushrooms just giggle beneath their seat.

Sunlight splashes like paint on a wall,
Every branch joins in a playful sprawl.
Breezes tickle the branches above,
Nature whispers secrets of silly love.

Laughter spills out when the day is done,
As fireflies dance, a laughable run.
So grab your hat and join the delight,
In this quirky world, everything feels right.

Stillness in a Blazing World

In a world so loud, the leaves just tease,
Wobbling in stillness with the greatest ease.
Acorns fall, making plops that resound,
While chipmunks are scouting for treasure unbound.

A bear jogs by in a tutu so grand,
Waving at trees that can't understand.
Pumpkins in patches are practicing cheer,
While squirrels prepare for a nutty career.

The sun's like an artist splashing on tan,
Barbecuing nature's great grilling plan.
With laughter echoing through every nook,
Even the shadows are learning to cook.

So hush for a moment, embrace the fun,
Nature's party has only begun.
With giggles and grins, we'll dance through the night,
Creating memories, oh what a sight!

Whirling Spirits of the Forest

Breezes swirl like dancers in a hall,
While mushrooms twirl, they are having a ball.
Leaves spiral down with a fluttering cheer,
Singing of laughter that we all hold dear.

Squirrels take bets on who'll climb the highest,
With a wink and a wink, they rally the shyest.
Wily raccoons play cards by moonlight,
With a deck made of shadows, they play all night.

The owls are judges with spectacles on,
Critiquing the waltz of the firefly dawn.
Even the roots show off their fine groove,
As the forest swings into rhythm and move.

Winds whisper tales that are precious and rare,
Nature's own laughter, filling the air.
So spin with the spirits, let joy take its course,
In this woodland wonder, we find our own force.

Between the Tree Trunks

Hidden laughter in the woods so thick,
As tree trunks gossip with each little trick.
Shadows dance like kids on a spree,
With the sun peeking out, as nosy as can be.

Bark-clad comedians share jokes and jests,
While busy bees fluff up their floral vests.
A raccoon in glasses reads jokes from a book,
And the bushes all giggle at the mischief they took.

Squirrels recite poetry, acorns in tow,
With a rhythmic beat that sets them aglow.
Underneath the canopy, mischief runs high,
As butterflies flutter by to say hi.

So come take a moment, peer into this space,
Where nature holds court, and there's laughter to chase.
Between every trunk, the fun is profound,
In this woodland wonder, happiness abounds.

www.ingramcontent.com/pod-product-compliance
Lightning Source LLC
Chambersburg PA
CBHW071830160426
43209CB00003B/259